Prepare your sails and get ready for an adventure with Captain Simon

Captain Simon is ready for a new sea adventure.
Help him get to his ship

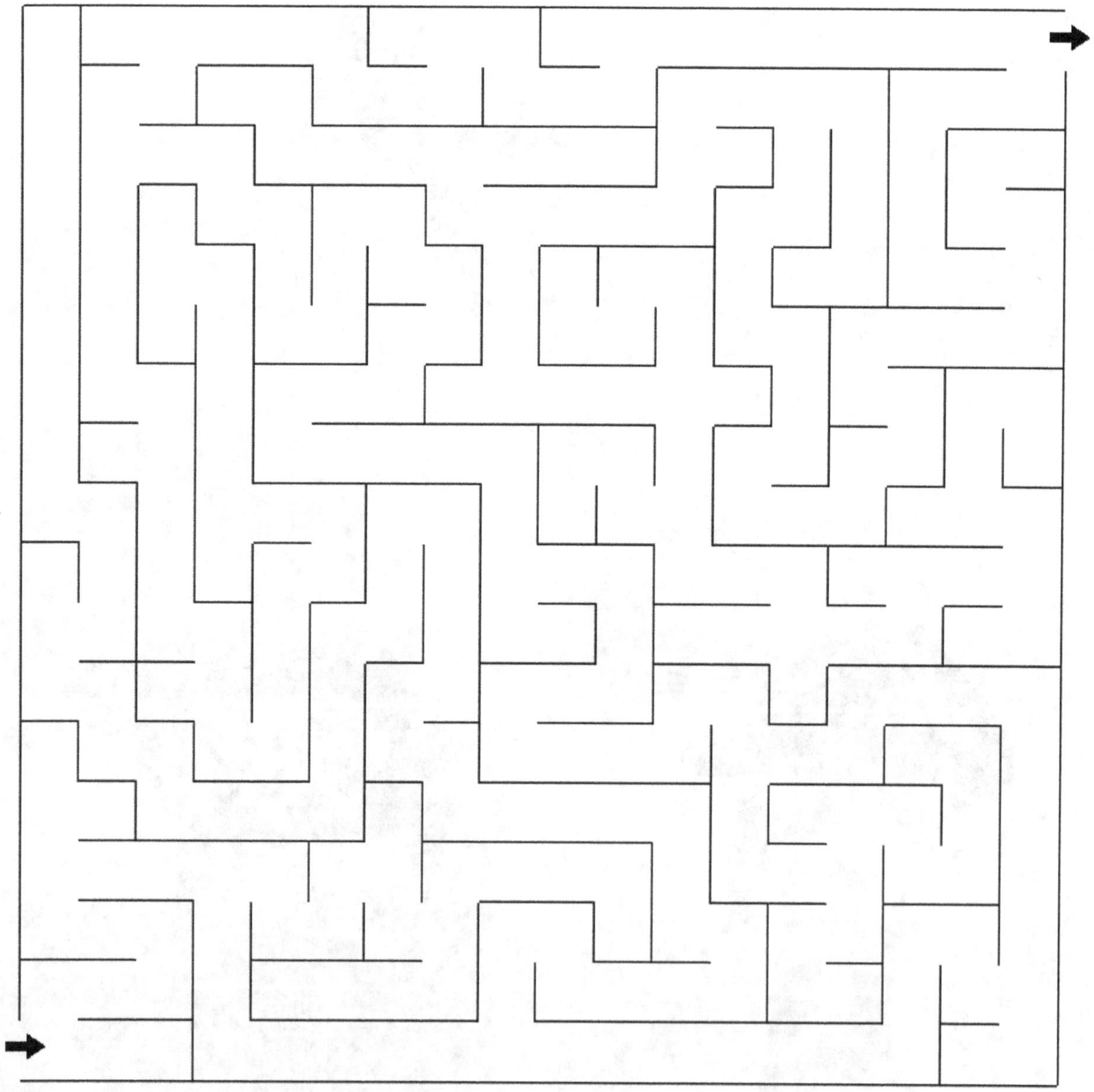

What about the rest of the crew? Lead Barry the Bearded and John the Young to the ship

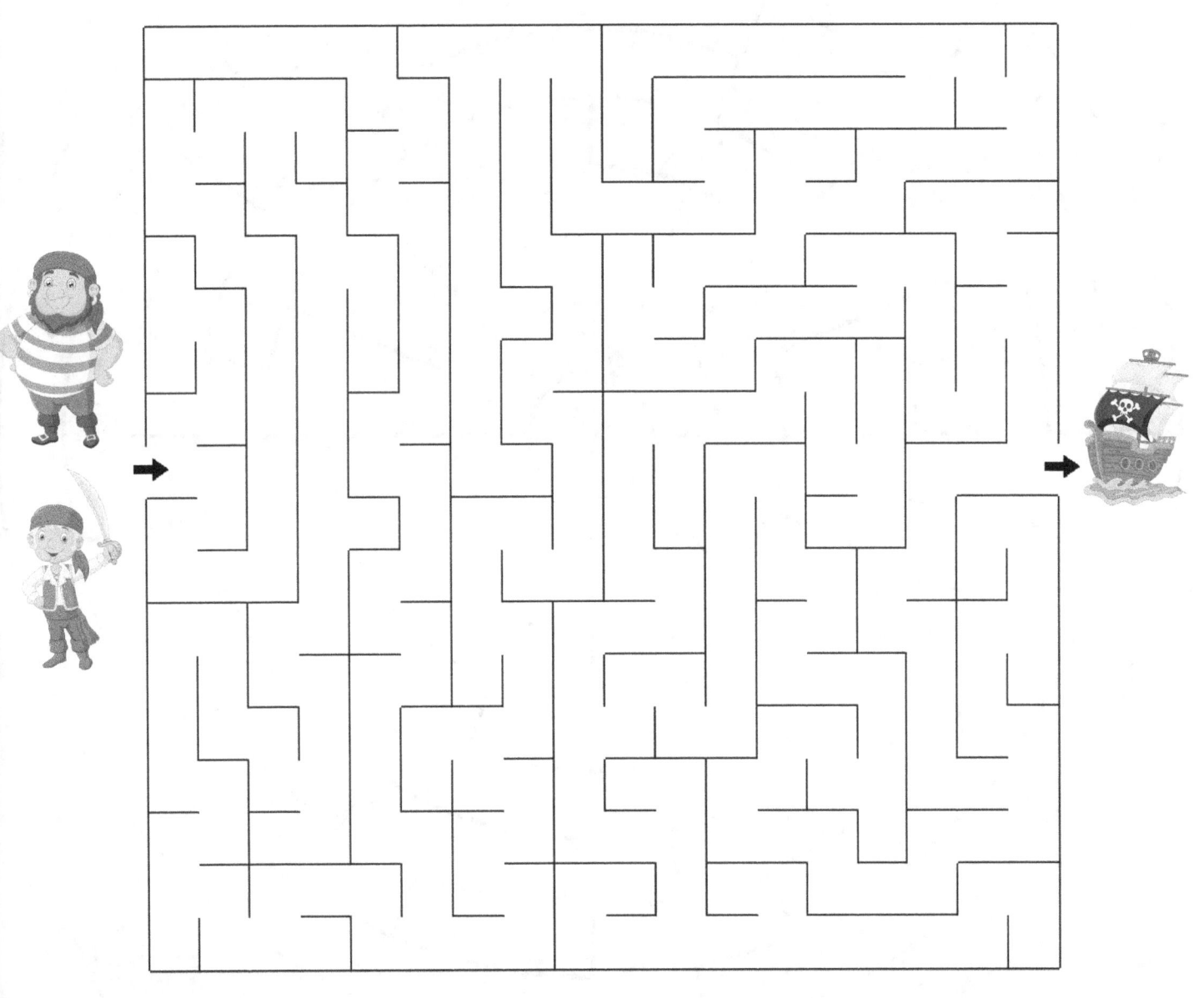

Don't forget Captain Simon's talking bird. Doctor Parrot get on board!

It looks like a message in a bottle. Get to the bottle, but be careful of the shark!

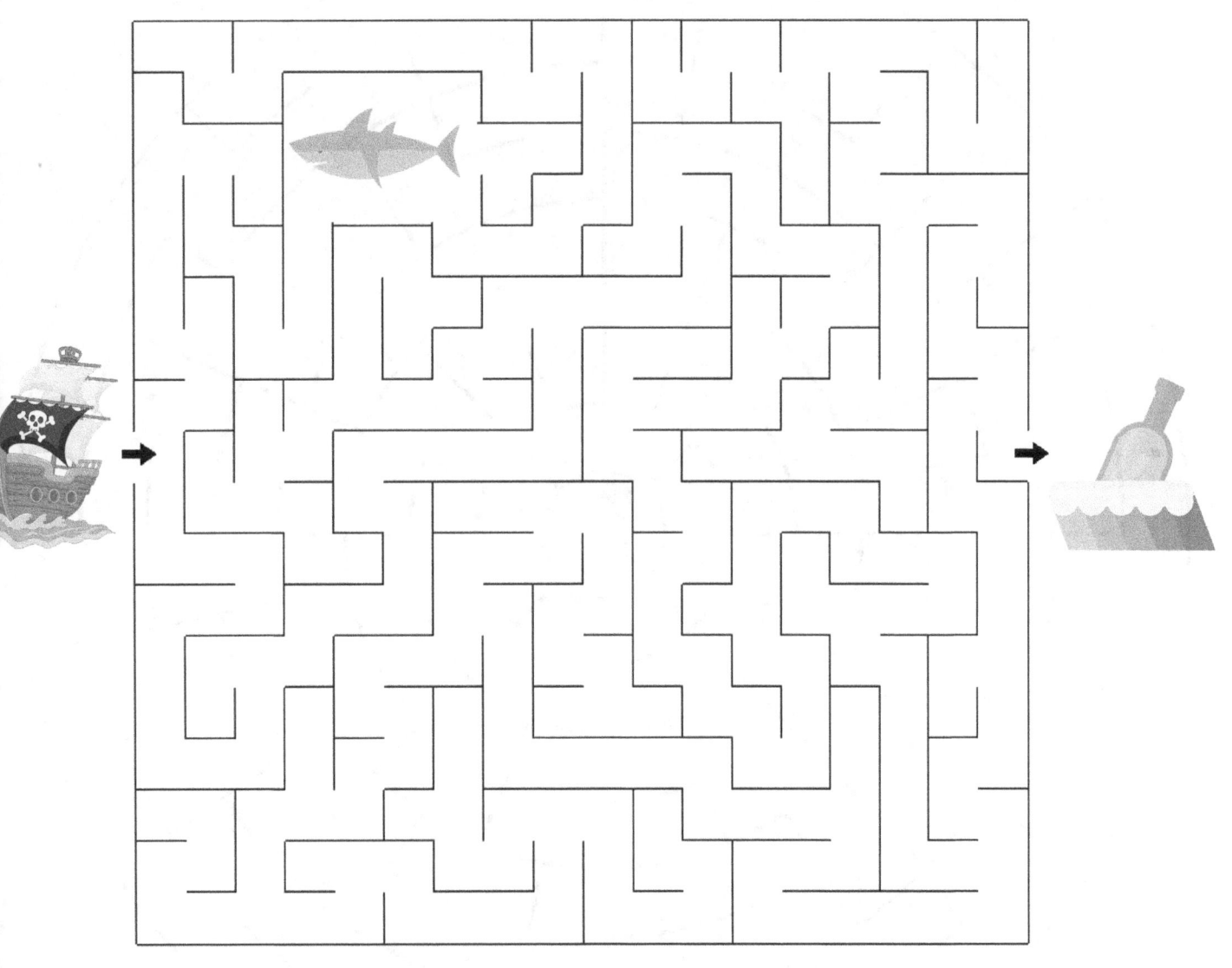

A map leading to a small Treasure Island was in the bottle. Help Captain Simon follow the map

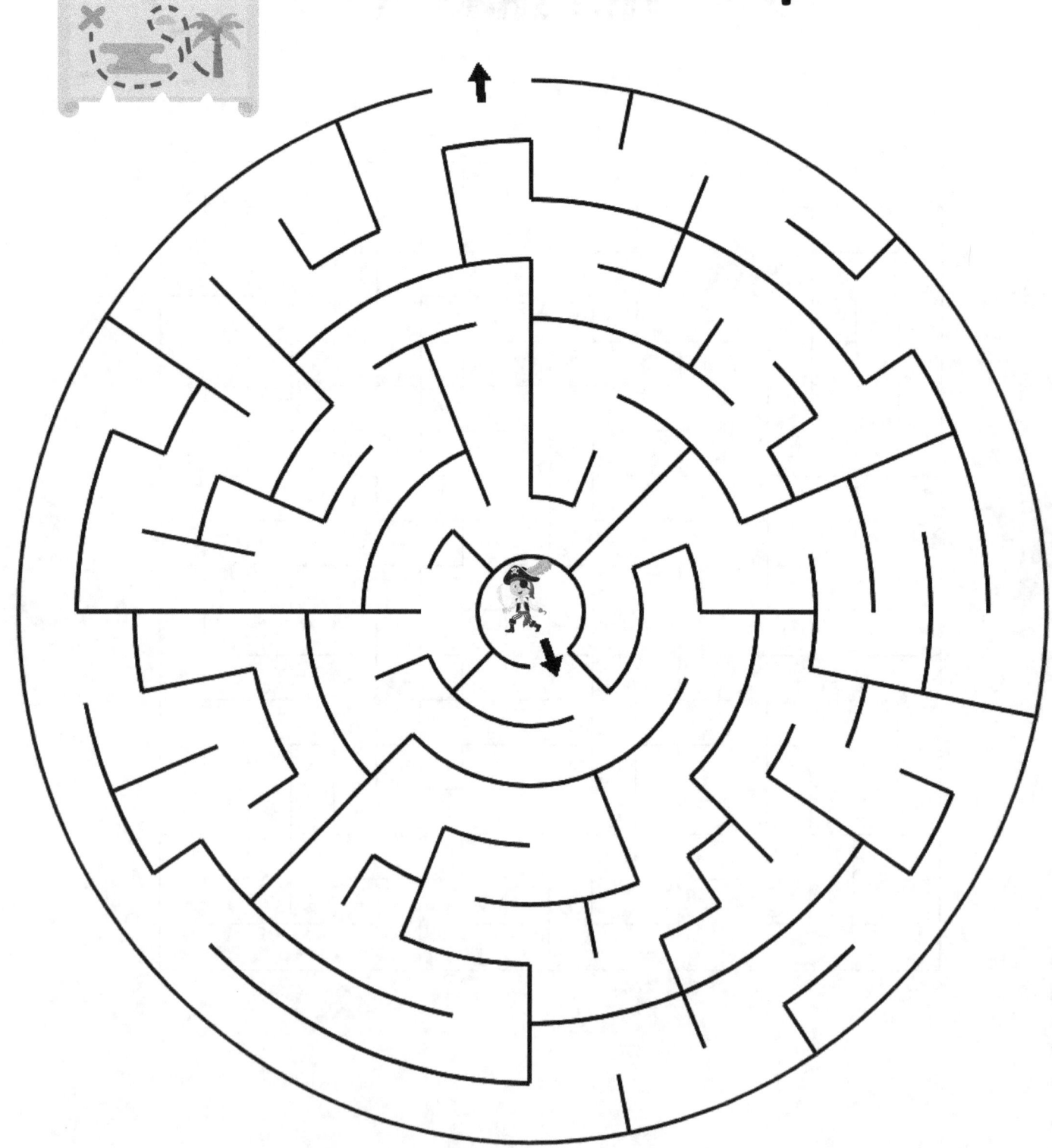

The treasure is in sight! Navigate through the rocks to claim the treasure

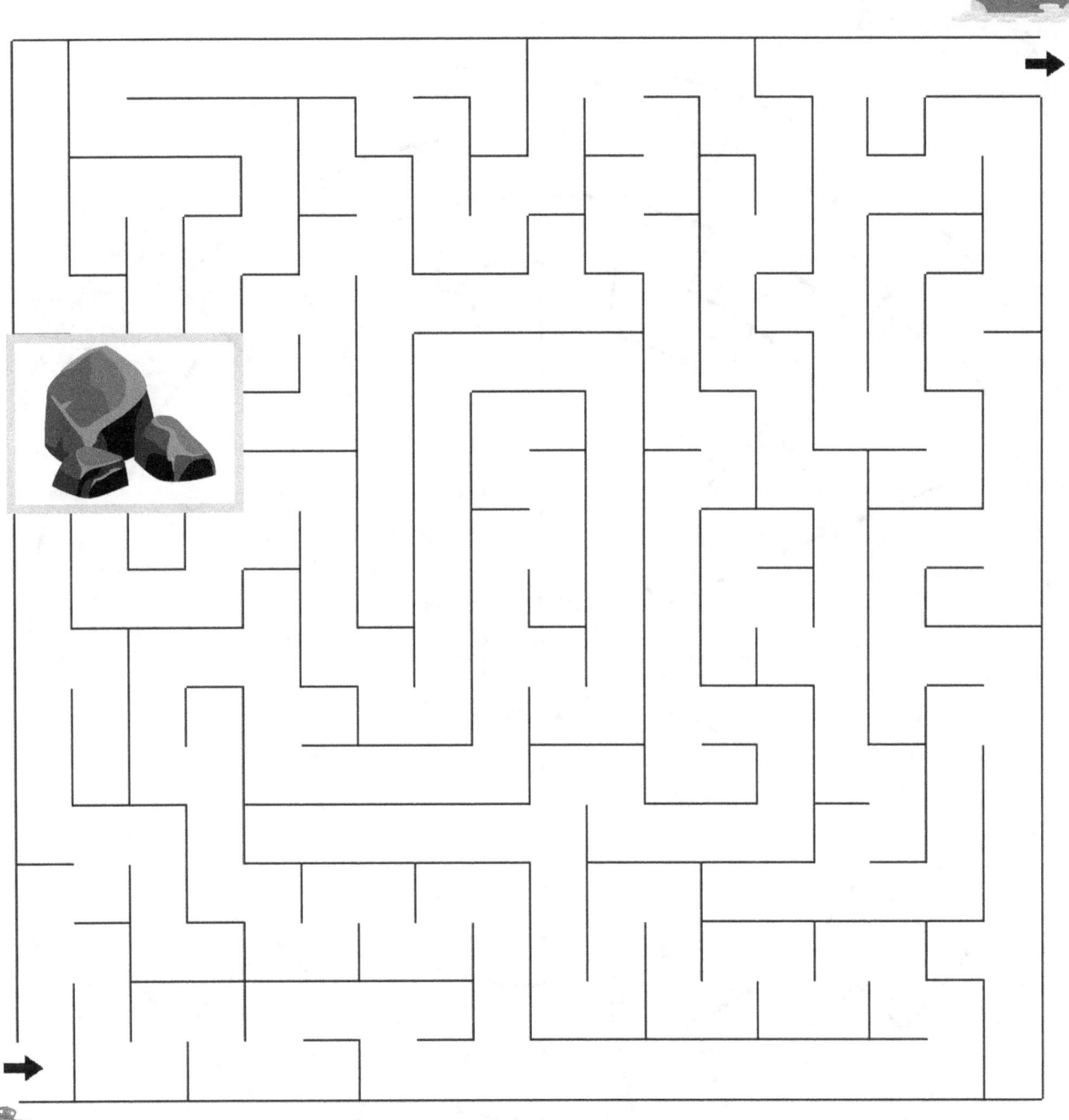

The crew is tired. Help them anchor for a while to take a rest

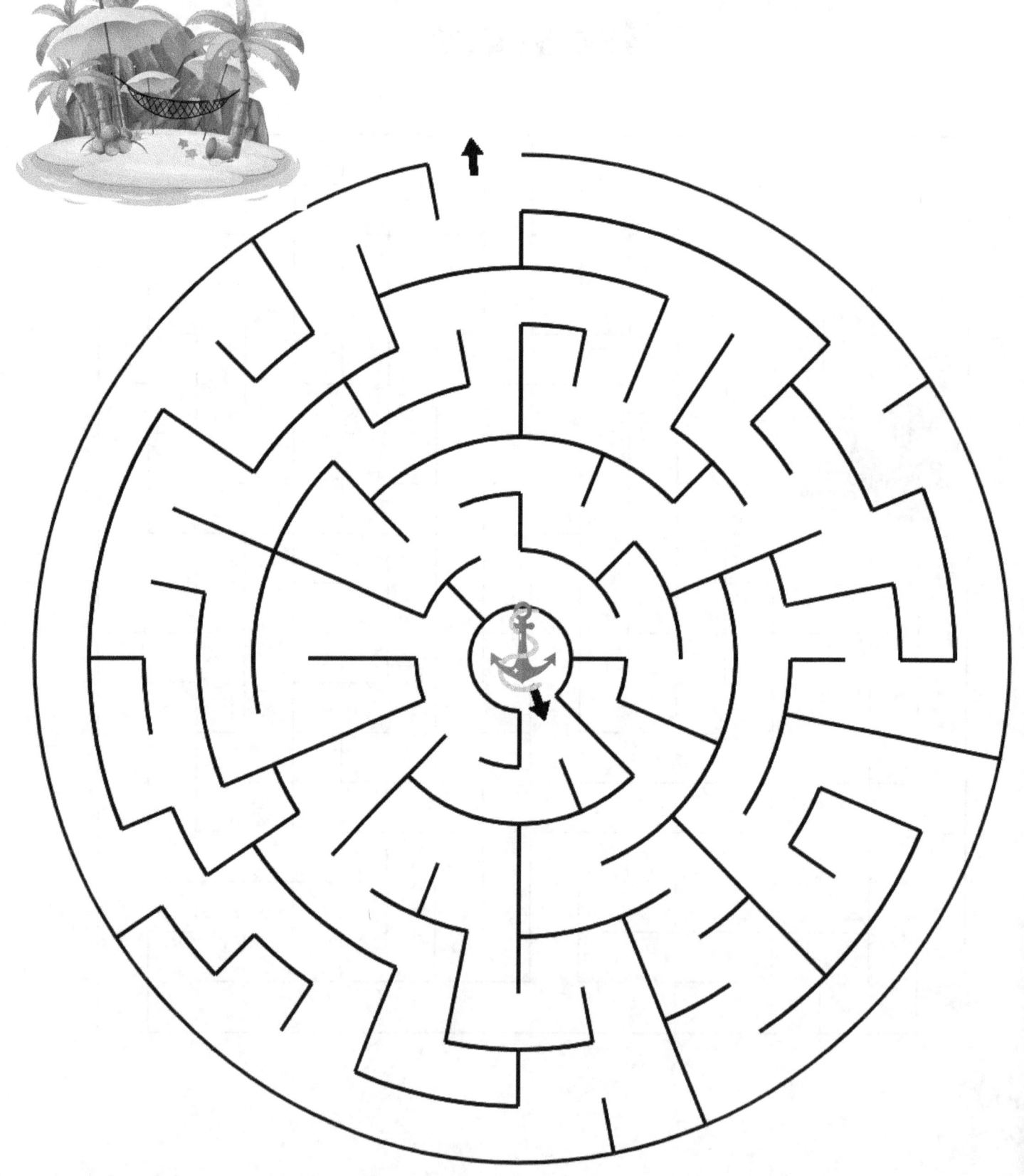

Captain Simon sees a ship flag in the distance.
Lead him there to have a closer look

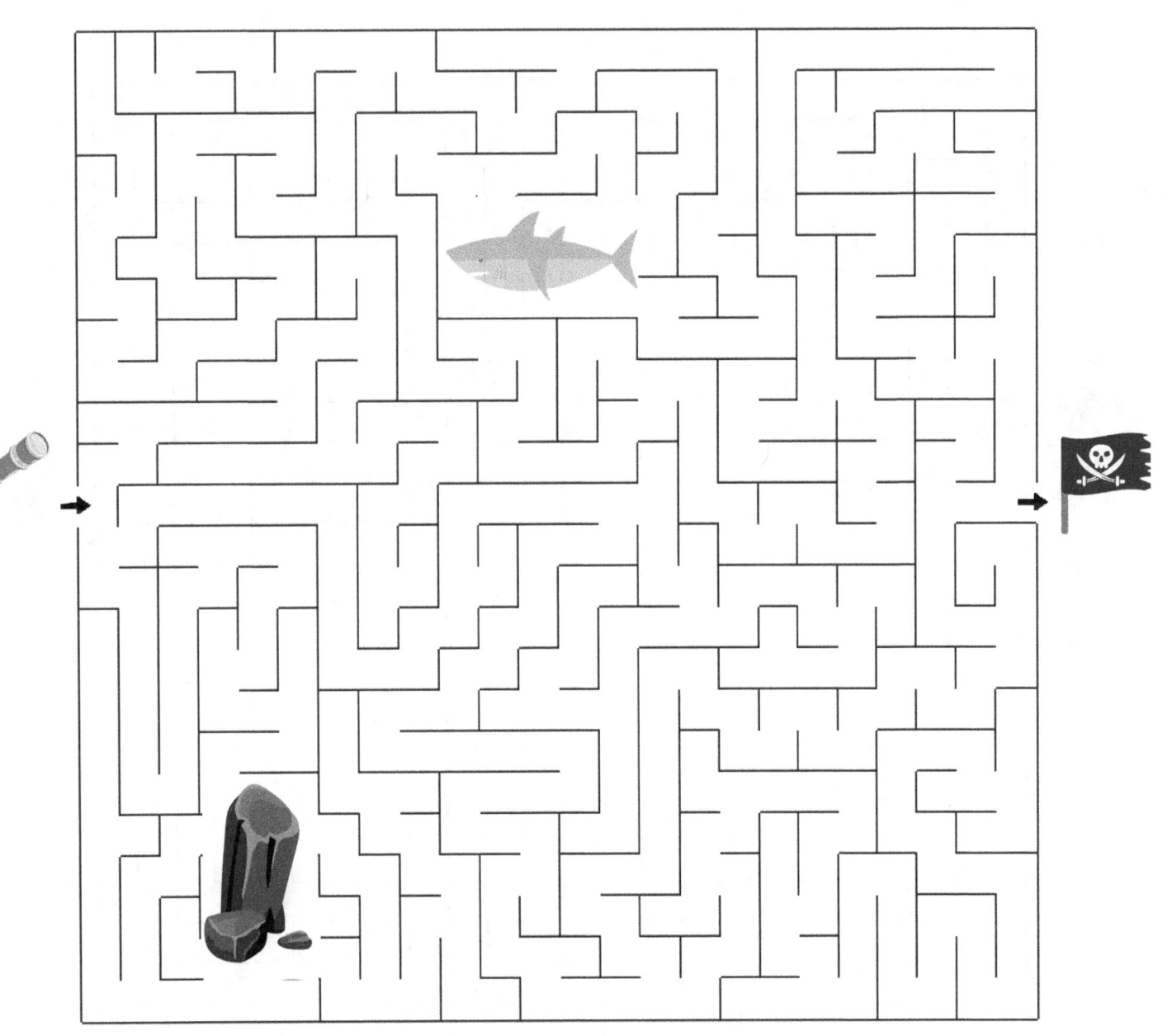

Oh, no! It's the flag of Captain Papageorge's ship, the evil pirate. Help Captain Simon and his crew steer their ship away

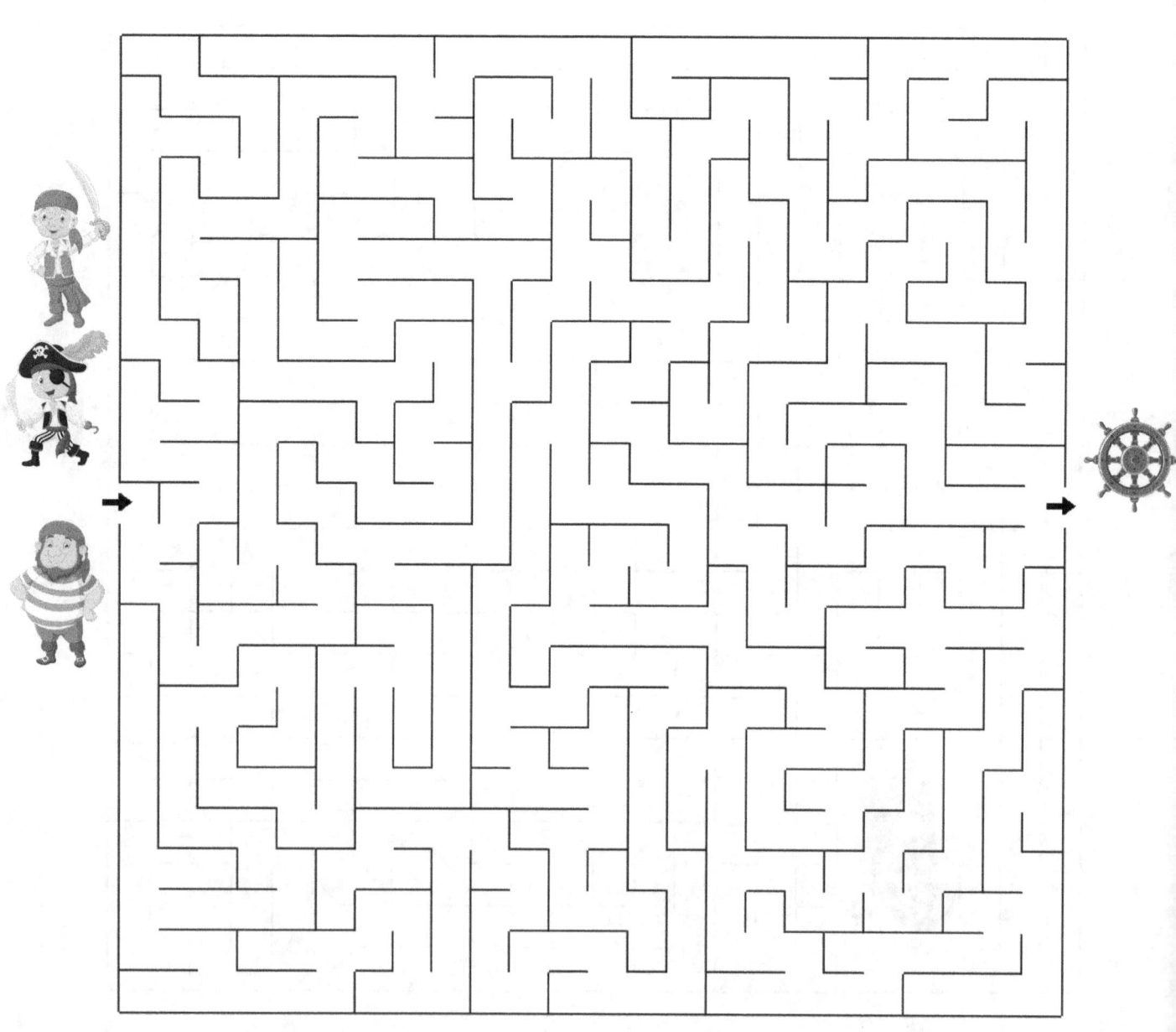

Evil Captain Papageorge has caught up. Help Barry the Bearded find his sword

Hooray! Captain Simon has won the battle, but he forgot the way to the Treasure Island. Help him get back

Doctor Parrot wants a refreshing swim in the sea. Help him get safely into the ship and avoid the sharks

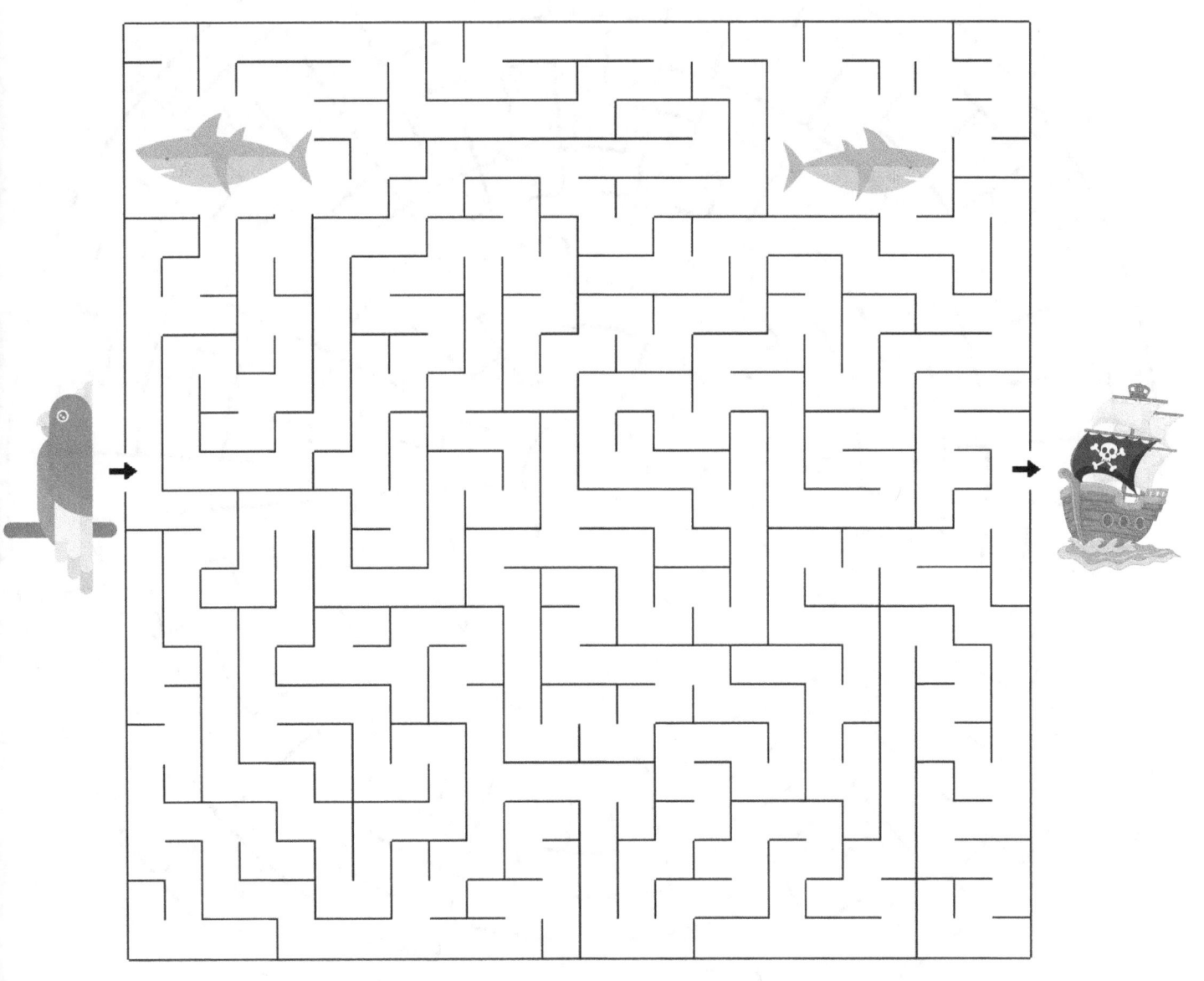

Captain Simon's crew is starving. Help them get a big fish for lunch

What about Doctor Parrot? He is starving too! Lead him to a nice piece of fruit

With a full belly, Captain Simon feels like napping. Help Captain Simon anchor to take another rest

Doctor Parrot has hidden the crew's boots! Find the boots before setting sail.

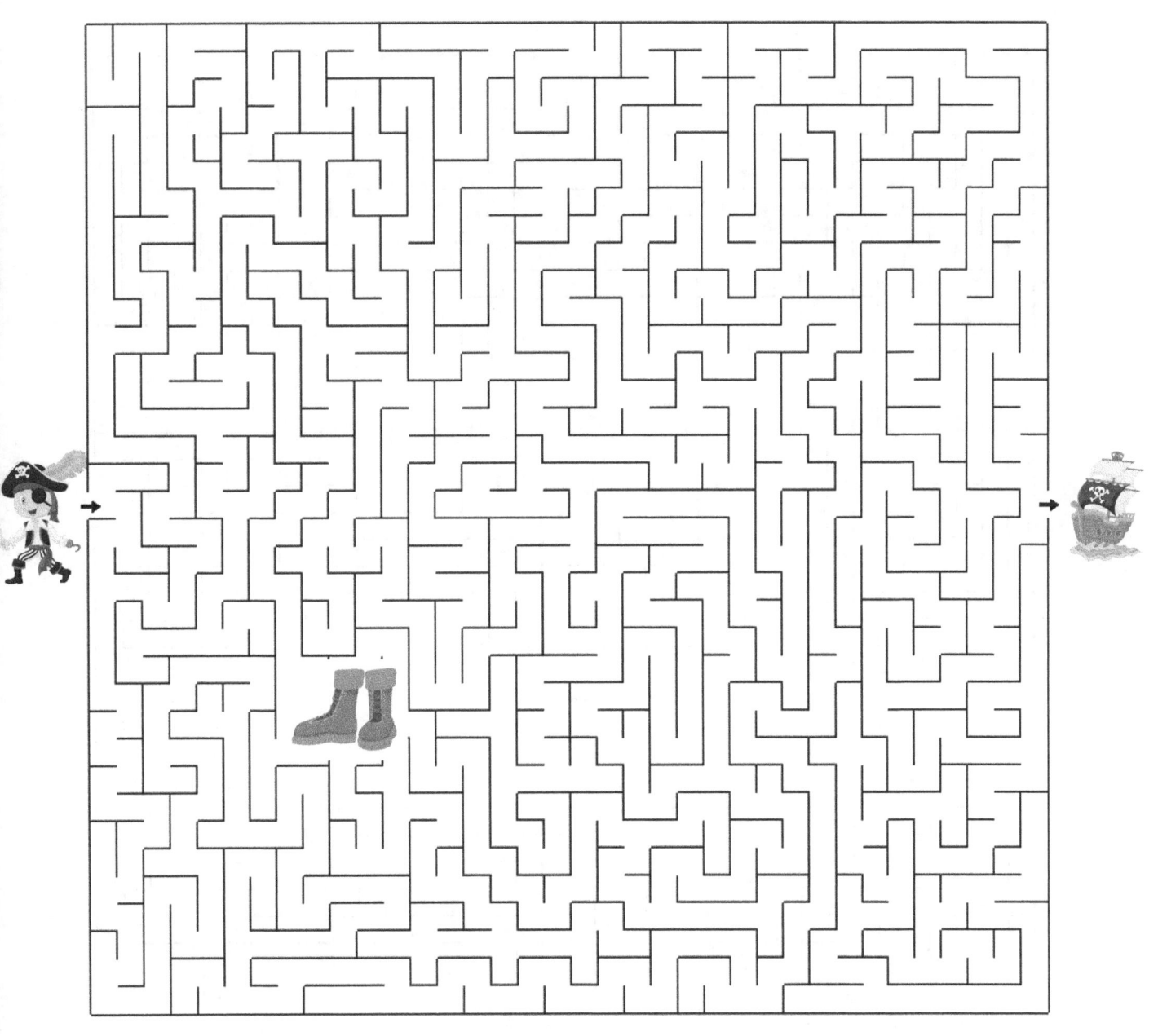

Doctor Parrot's friend Tiki is approaching. Help Tiki navigate through the winds to the ship.

Tiki warns of a nearby evil pirate ship. Get your crew back to the safety of a nearby town

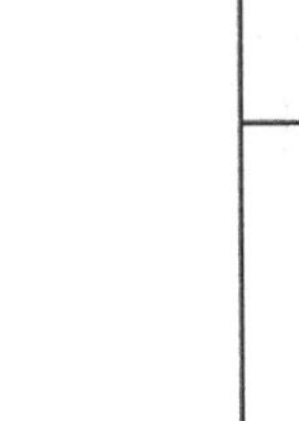

The locals are frightened of the sharks by the dock. Help Captain Simon get the fishing net and capture the sharks

The locals are thankful you cleared the docks. As a reward Captain Simon has been given a treasure map. Follow the map to the Island of Skulls

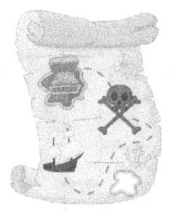

The map shows the treasure is on top of the highest mountain. Go there

I can see the treasure chest shining from here, but what about that guardian dragon? Avoid it to get to the treasure chest

Let's get the tools to dig up the treasure

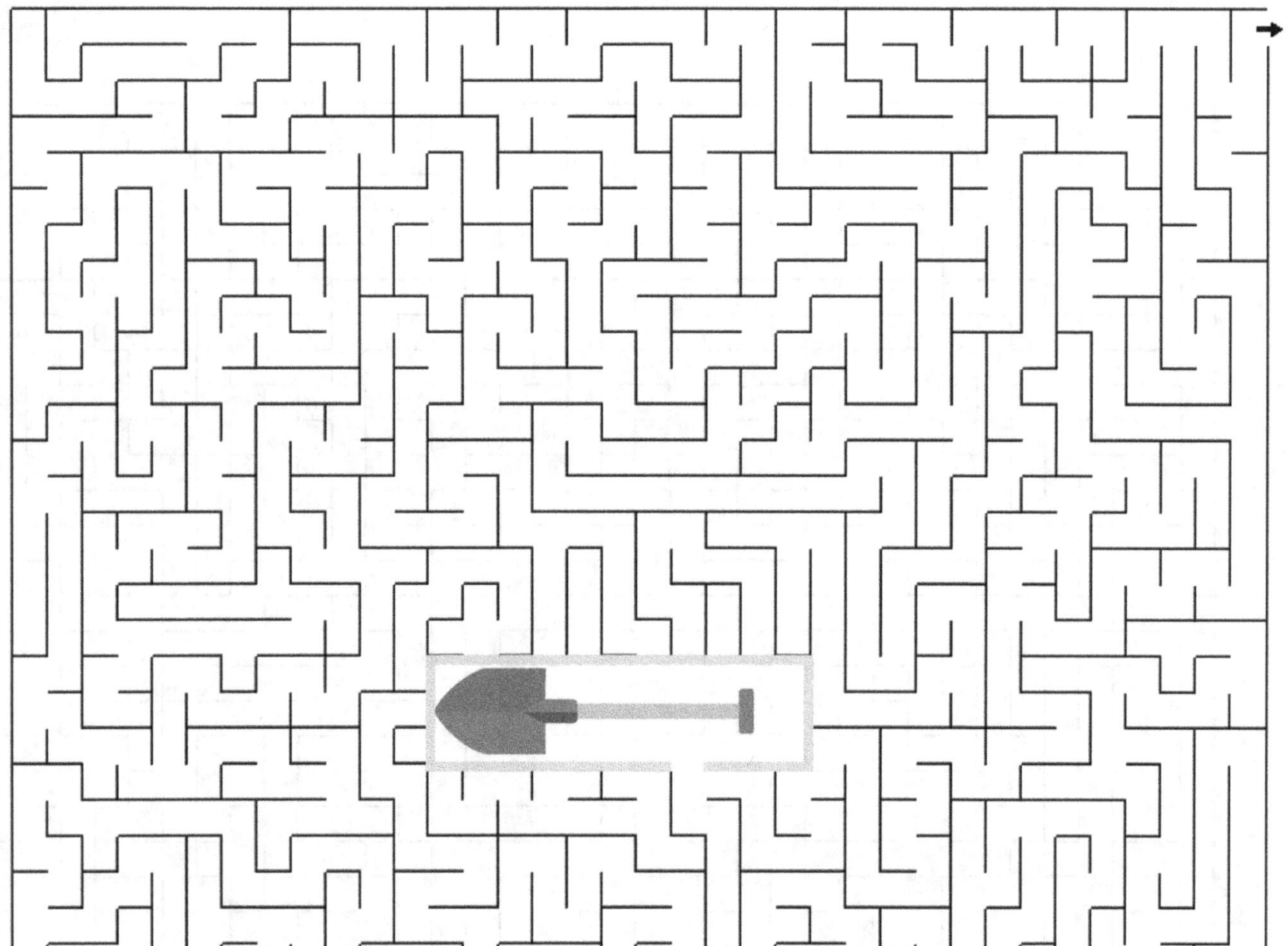

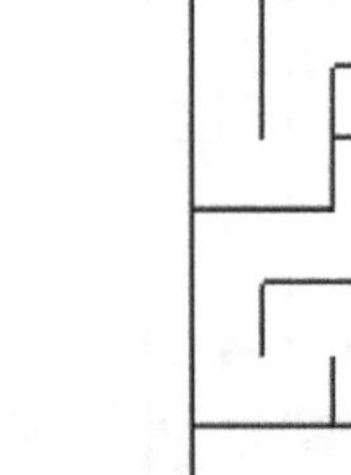

Help Captain Simon put the treasure into his bag

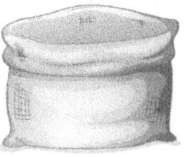

What's that ?! The ground is shaking ! A nearby volcano is erupting ! Carry the treasure back to the ship

Sail the ship safely away from the volcano

The crew can't decide whether to go home or find more treasure. Find a coin to make the decision

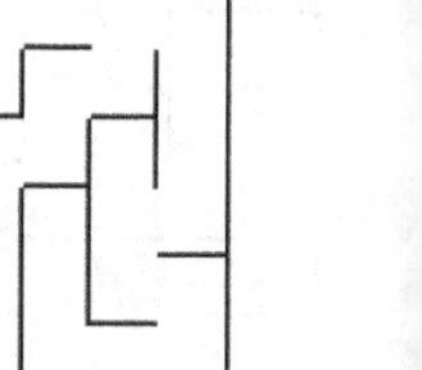

Whilst looking for a coin in the treasure, the crew discovered a cursed skull. Find Fiona the fortune teller to learn how to destroy it

Fiona says those who carry the skull are destined to bad luck. The only way to destroy it is with an enchanted sword from Skeleton Island. Get to the island

Fiona said the enchanted sword is deep in the center of a lake on the island. Swim to the bottom. Avoid the giant octopus

Well done ! The skull is destroyed and the curse lifted ! Follow the compass home

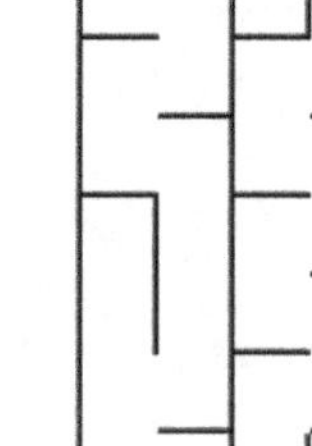

The seas are rough. Steer through the waves to return home

Captain Simon is ready for a new sea adventure. Help him get to his ship

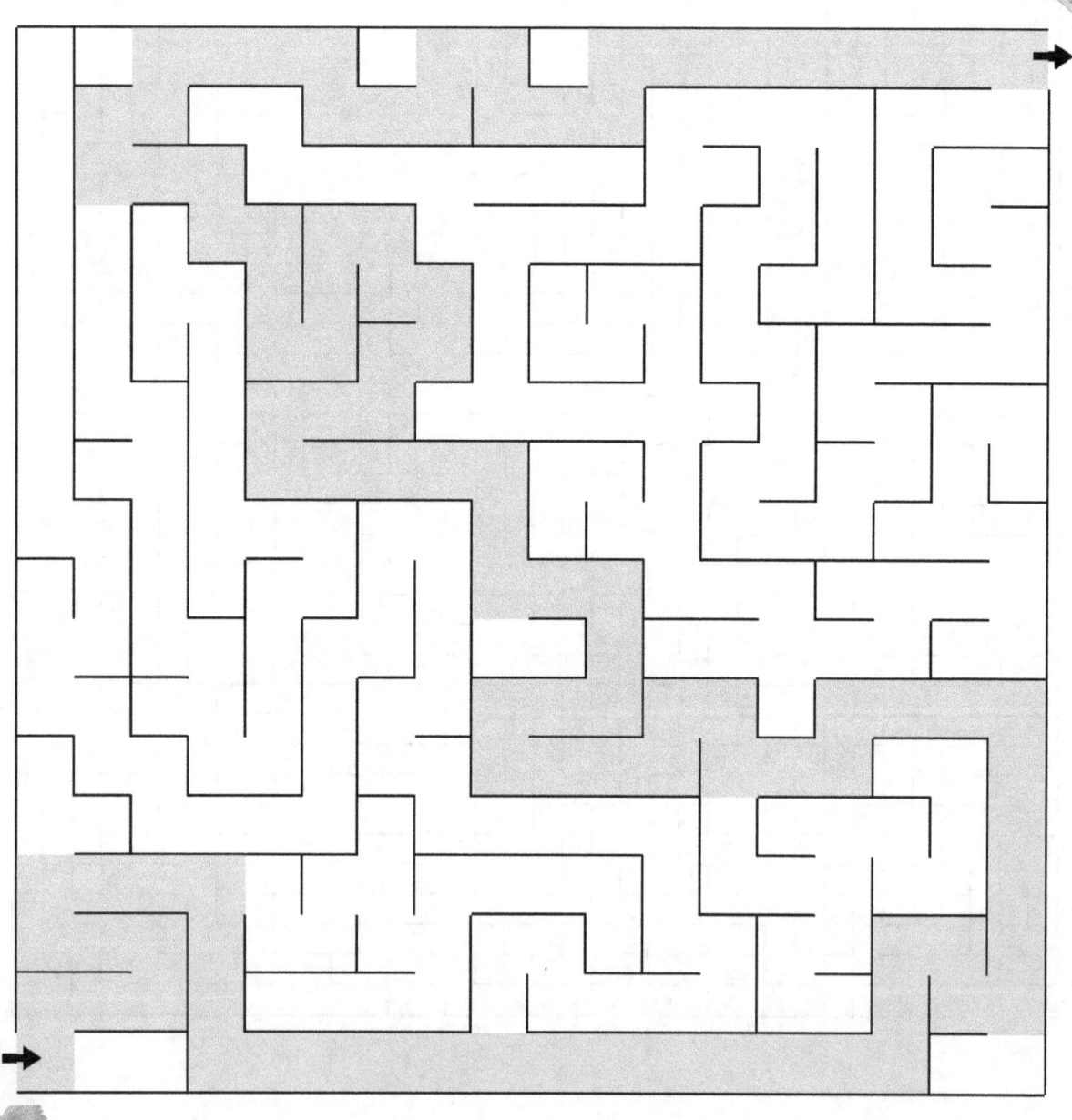

What about the rest of the crew? Lead Barry the Bearded and John the Young to the ship

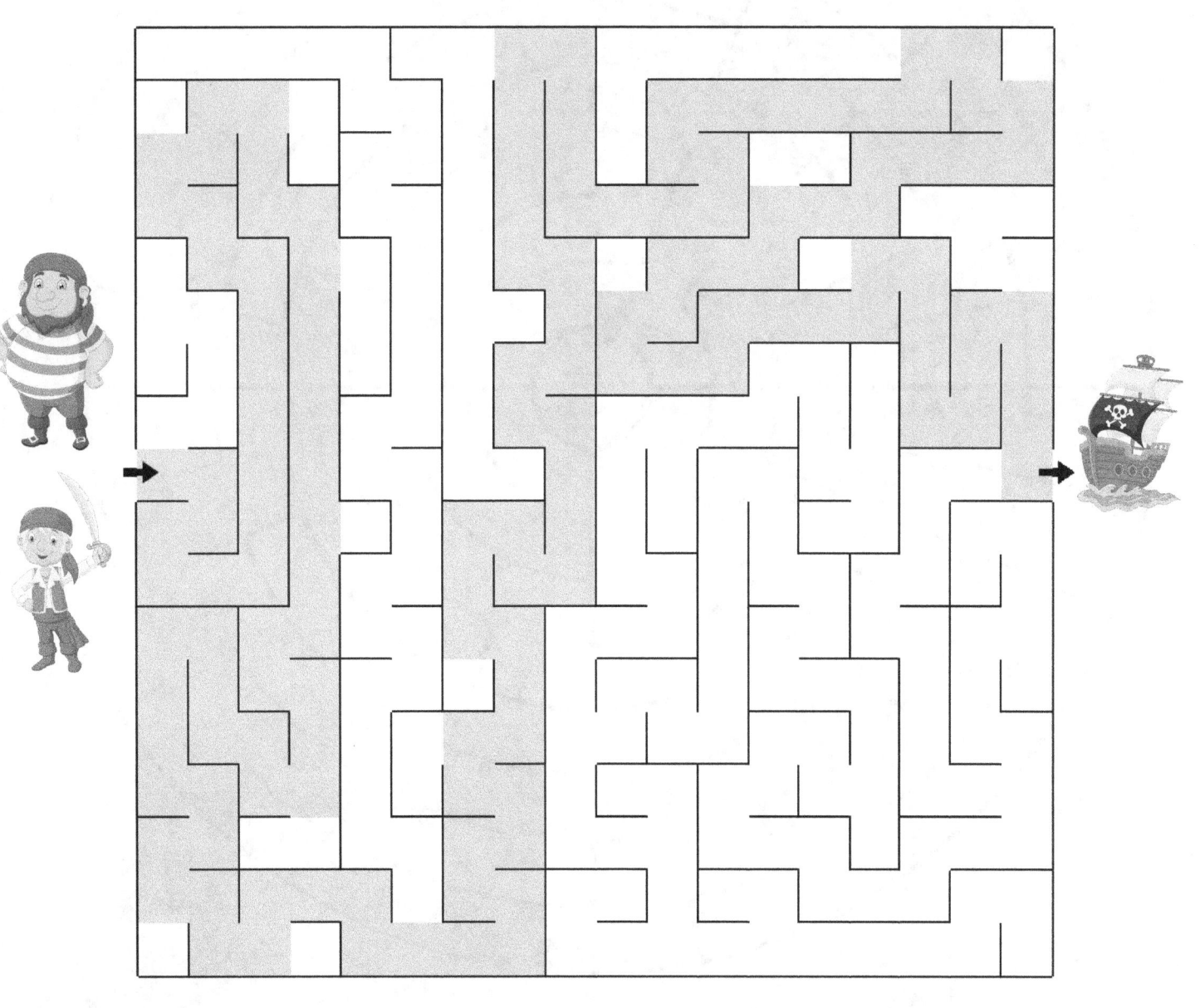

Don't forget Captain Simon's talking bird. Doctor Parrot get on board!

It looks like a message in a bottle. Get to the bottle, but be careful of the shark!

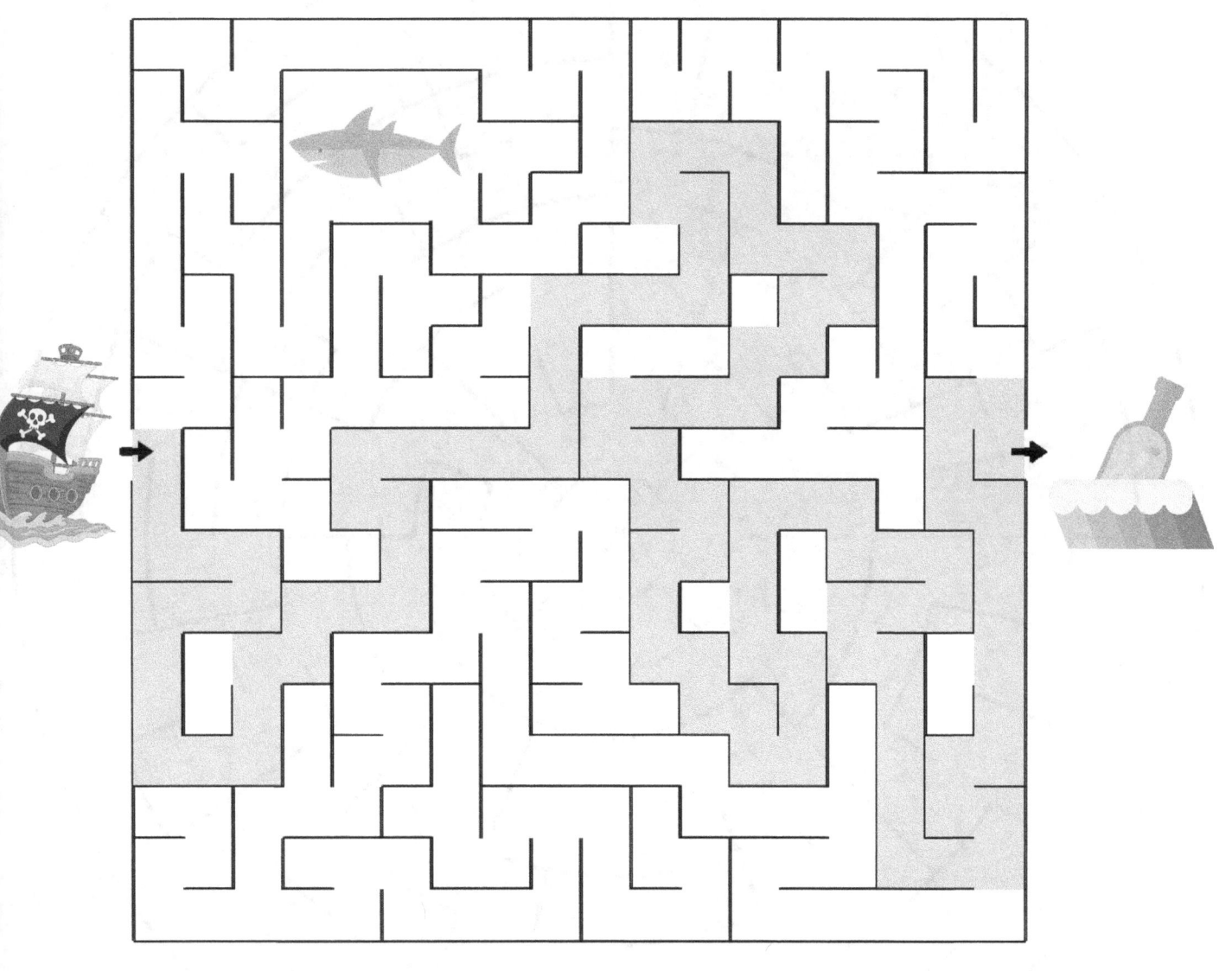

A map leading to a small Treasure Island was in the bottle. Help Captain Simon follow the map

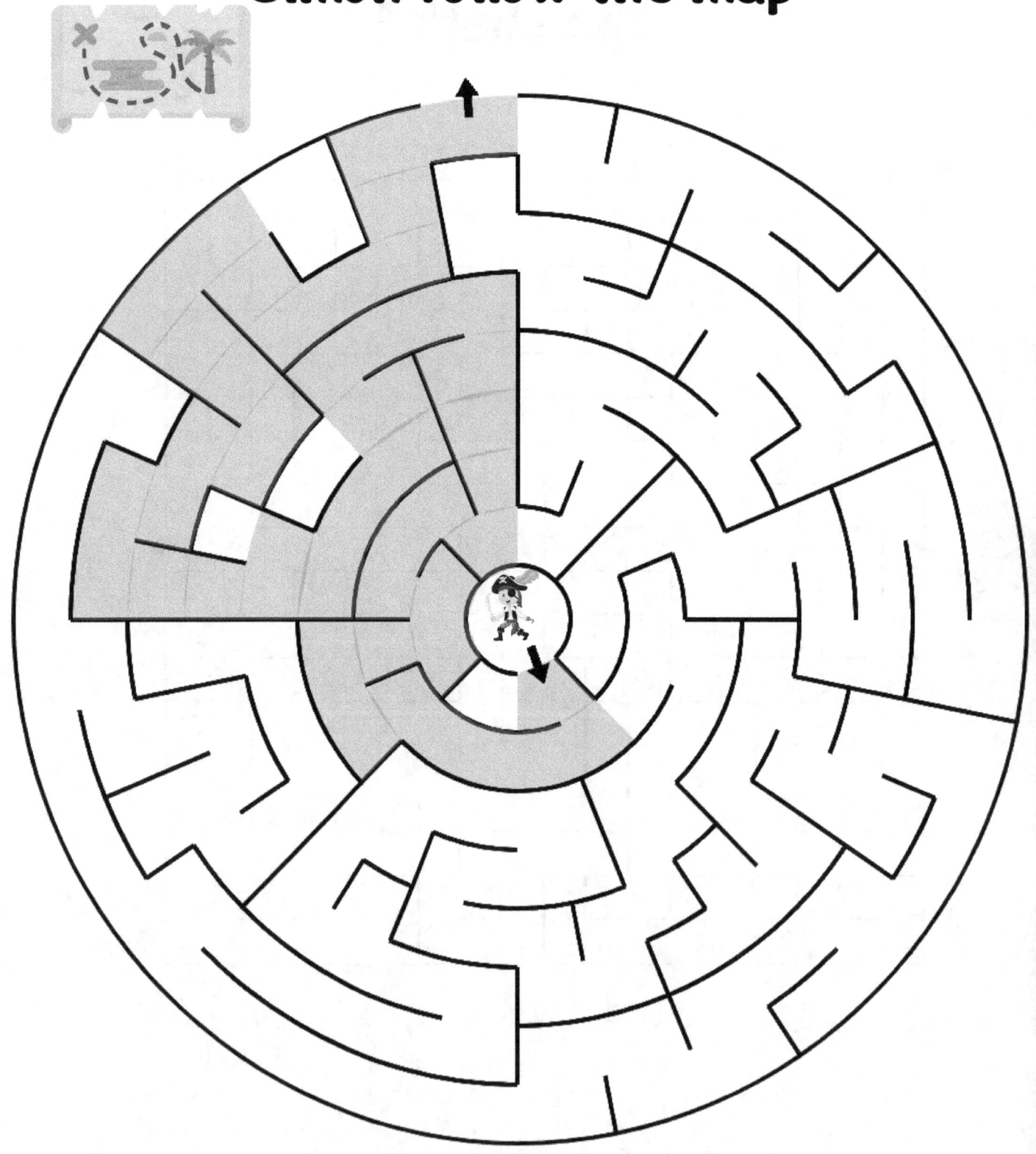

The treasure is in sight! Navigate through the rocks to claim the treasure

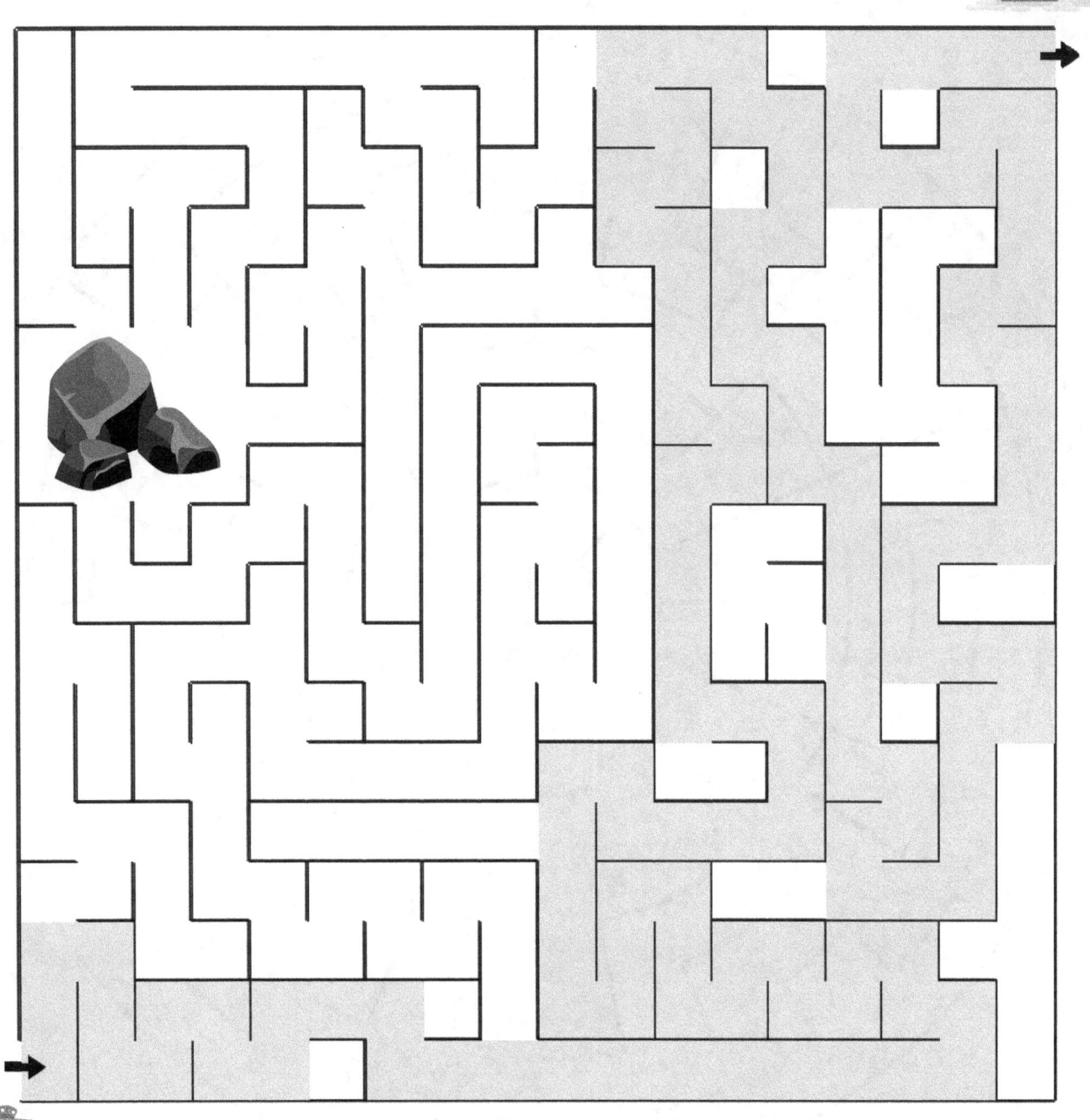

The crew is tired. Help them anchor for a while to take a rest

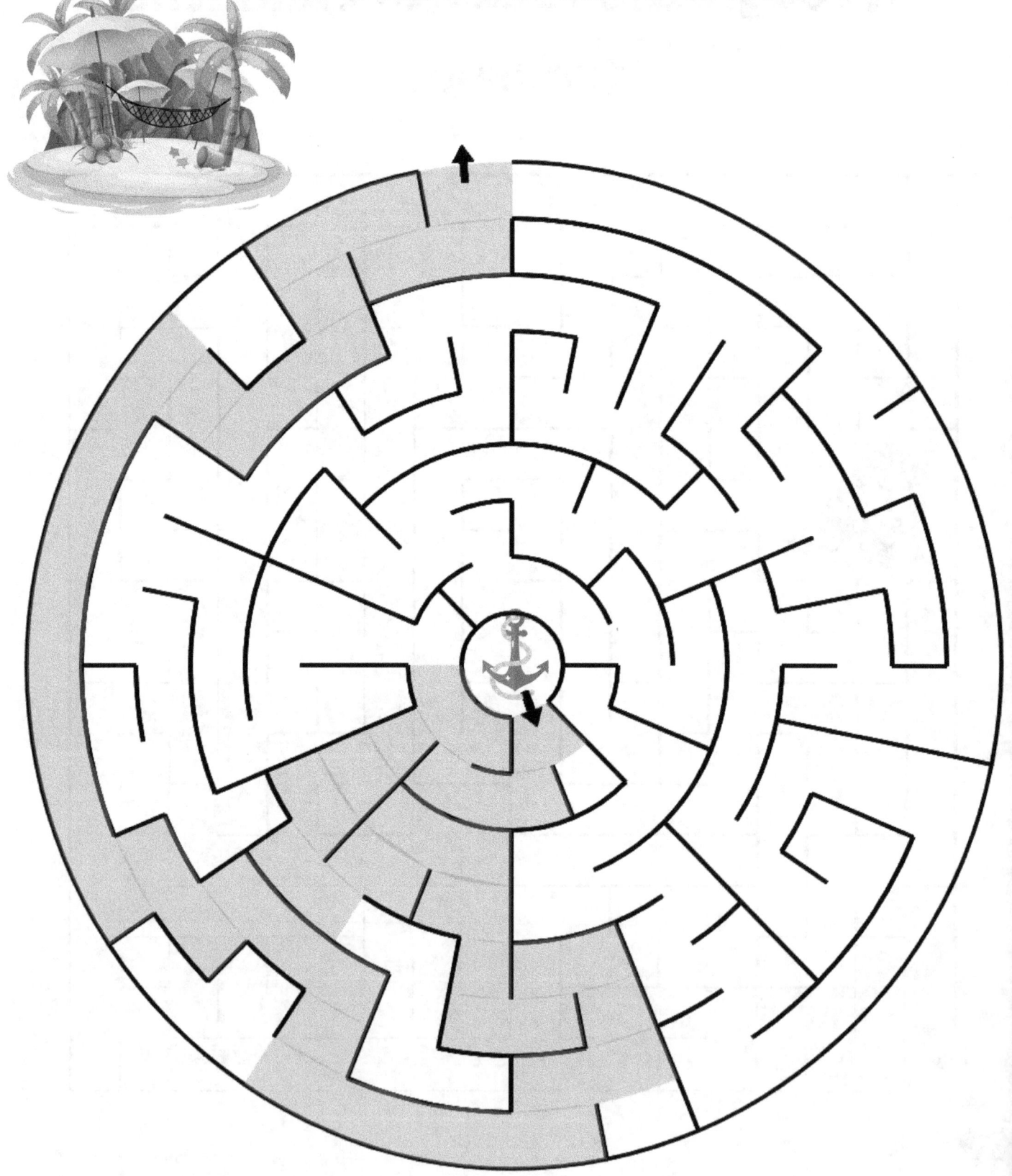

Captain Simon sees a ship flag in the distance.
Lead him there to have a closer look

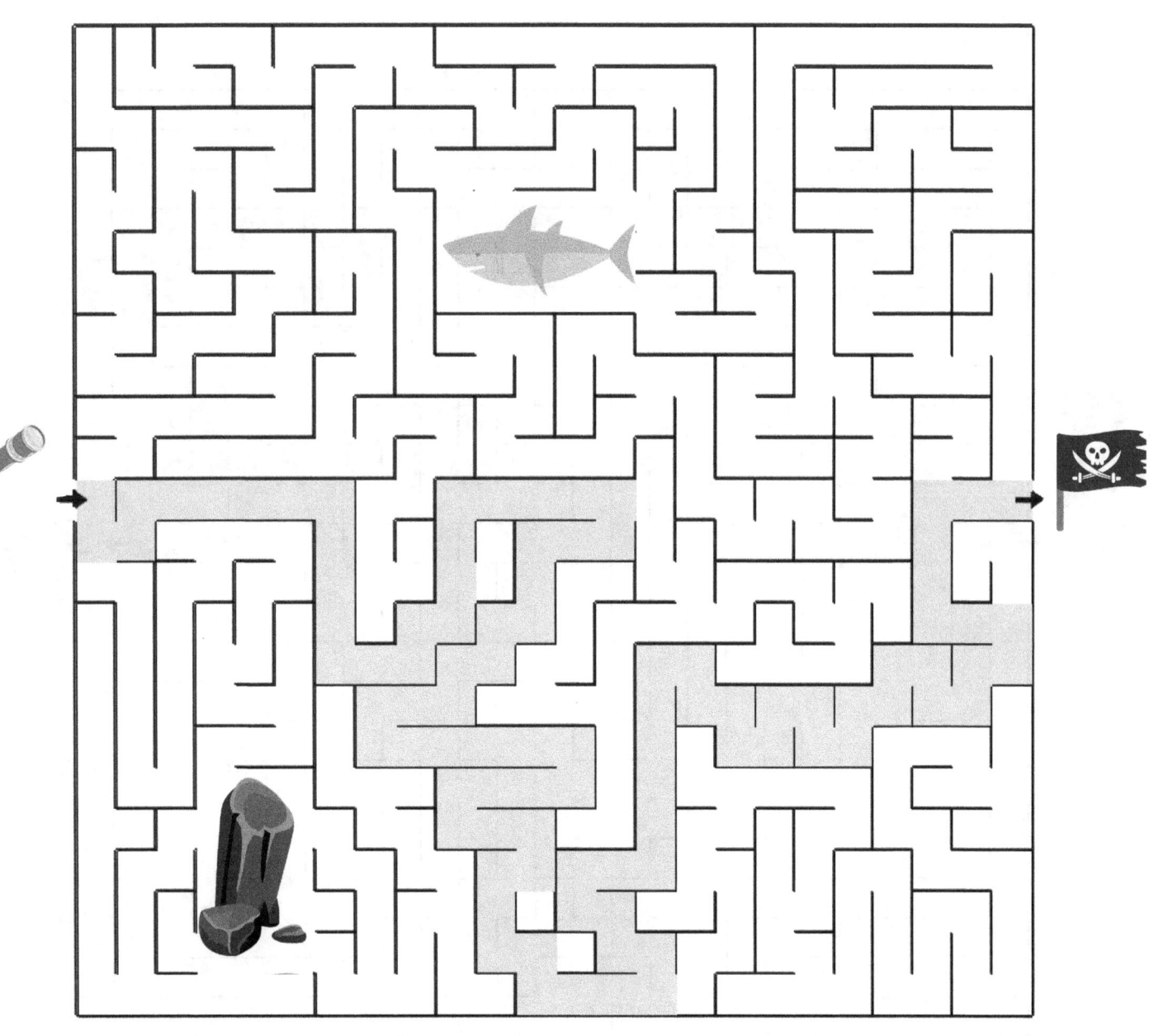

Oh, no! It's the flag of Captain Papageorge's ship, the evil pirate. Help Captain Simon and his crew steer their ship away

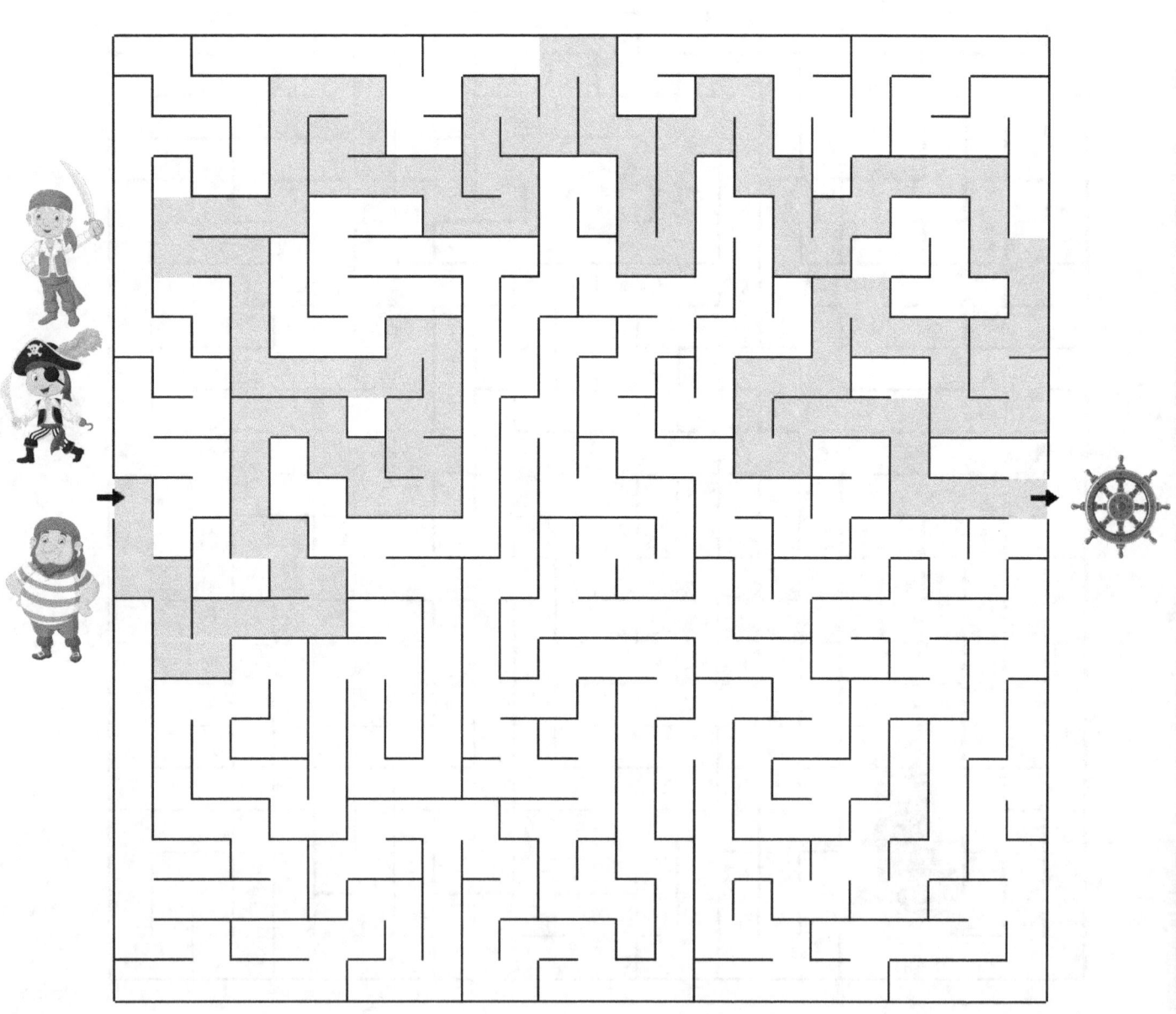

Evil Captain Papageorge has caught up. Help Barry the Bearded find his sword

Hooray! Captain Simon has won the battle, but he forgot the way to the Treasure Island. Help him get back

Doctor Parrot wants a refreshing swim in the sea. Help him get safely into the ship and avoid the sharks

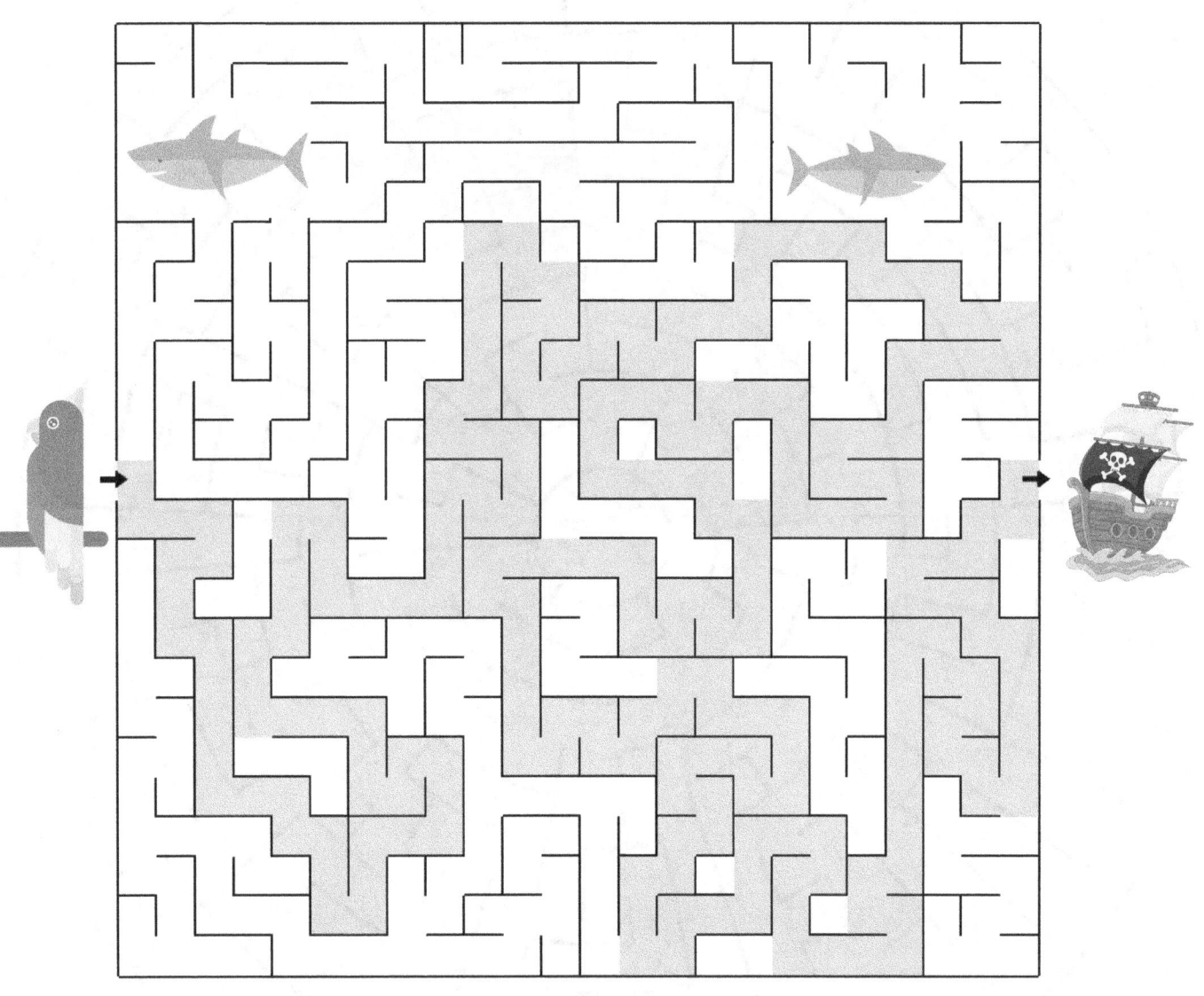

Captain Simon's crew is starving. Help them get a big fish for lunch

What about Doctor Parrot? He is starving too! Lead him to a nice piece of fruit

With a full belly, Captain Simon feels like napping. Help Captain Simon anchor to take another rest

Doctor Parrot has hidden the crew's boots! Find the boots before setting sail.

Doctor Parrot's friend Tiki is approaching. Help Tiki navigate through the winds to the ship.

Tiki warns of a nearby evil pirate ship. Get your crew back to the safety of a nearby town

The locals are frightened of the sharks by the dock. Help Captain Simon get the fishing net and capture the sharks

The locals are thankful you cleared the docks. As a reward Captain Simon has been given a treasure map. Follow the map to the Island of Skulls

The map shows the treasure is on top of the highest mountain. Go there

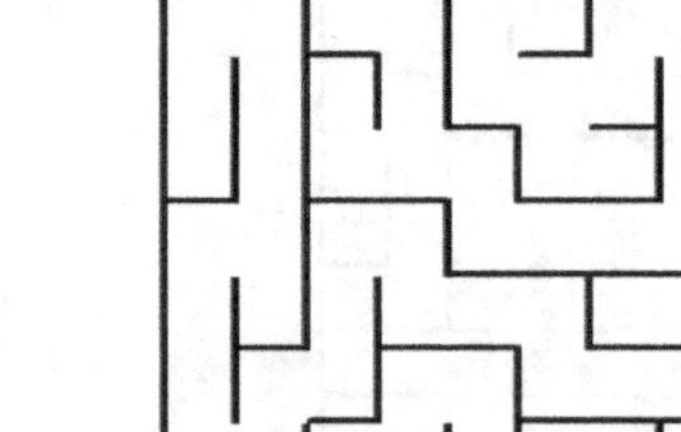

I can see the treasure chest shining from here, but what about that guardian dragon? Avoid it to get to the treasure chest

Let's get the tools to dig up the treasure

Help Captain Simon put the treasure into his bag

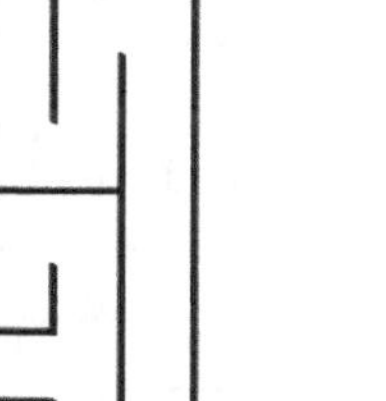

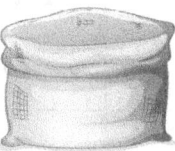

What's that?! The ground is shaking! A nearby volcano is erupting! Carry the treasure back to the ship

Sail the ship safely away from the volcano

The crew can't decide whether to go home or find more treasure. Find a coin to make the decision

Whilst looking for the coin in the treasure, the crew discovered a cursed skull. Find Fiona the fortune teller to learn how to destroy it

Fiona says those who carry the skull are destined to bad luck. The only way to destroy it is with an enchanted sword from Skeleton Island. Get to the island

Fiona said the enchanted sword is deep in the center of a lake on the island. Swim to the bottom. Avoid the giant octopus

Well done ! The skull is destroyed and the curse lifted ! Follow the compass home

The seas are rough. Steer through the waves to return home

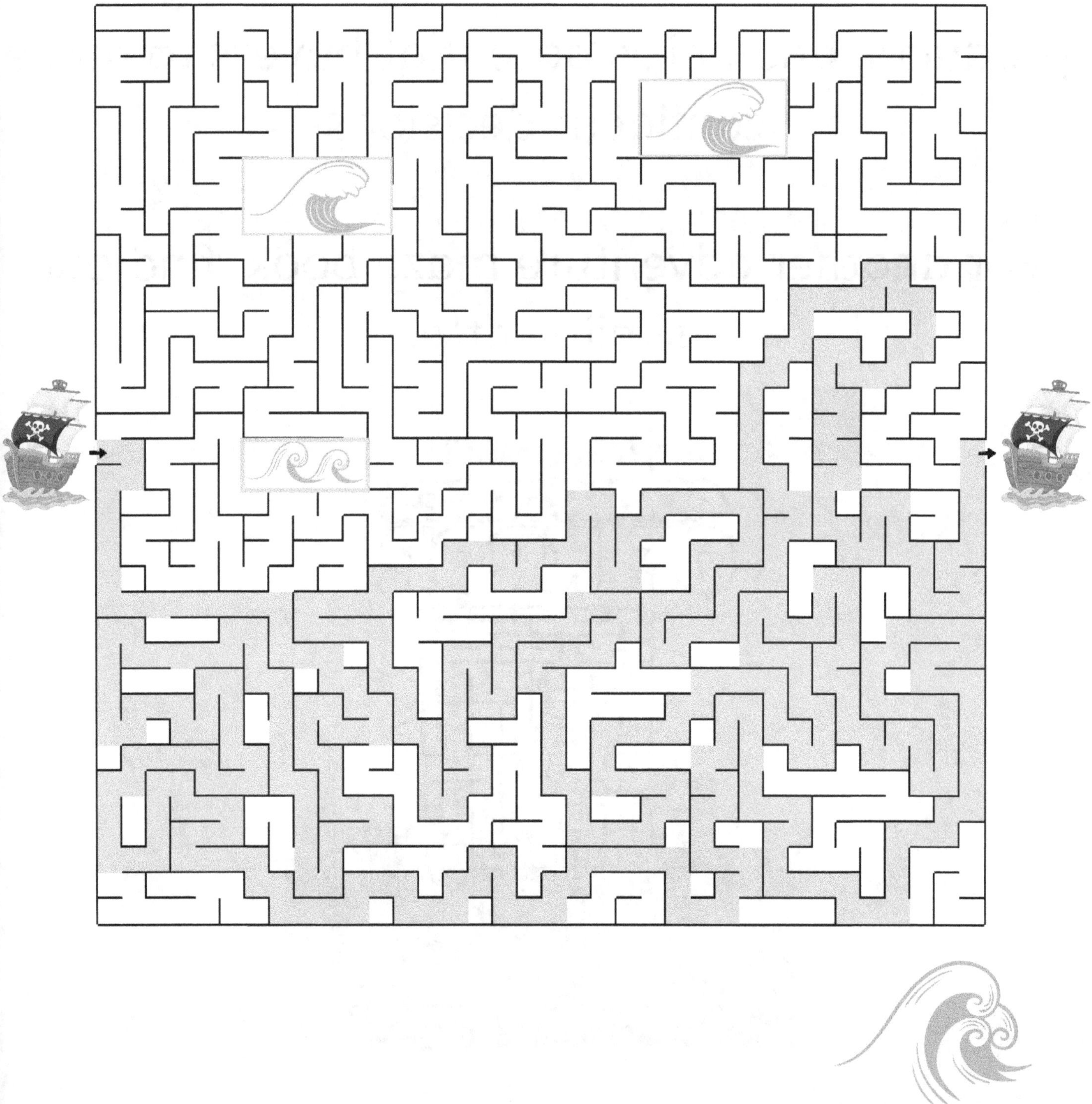

We hope you loved the mazes. If you did, would you consider posting an online review?

This helps us to continue providing great products, and helps potential buyers to make confident decisions.

For another adventure maze book, find our similar title:

www.ingramcontent.com/pod-product-compliance
Lightning Source LLC
Chambersburg PA
CBHW081236080526
44587CB00022B/3959